—

EASY-TO-COOK

STIR FRIES

Lyn Rutherford

BROCKHAMPTON PRESS
LONDON

First published in Great Britain in 1992 by
Anaya Publishers Ltd,
Strode House, 44–50 Osnaburgh Street, London NW1 3ND

This edition published 1996 by Brockhampton Press,
a member of Hodder Headline PLC Group

Managing Editor: Janet Illsley
Photographer: Alan Newnham
Designer: Pedro Prá-Lopez
Food Stylist: Lyn Rutherford
Background Artist: Sue Russell

British Library Cataloguing in Publication Data
Rutherford, Lyn
Easy to cook stir fries. – (Easy to cook)

ISBN 1 86019 230 0

Typeset in UK by SX Composing Ltd, Rayleigh
Colour reproduction by J. Film Process, Bangkok
Printed in UK by BPC Paulton Books Ltd

NOTES

Ingredients are listed in metric and imperial measures.
Use either set of quantities but not a mixture of both.

All spoon measures are level:
1 tablespoon = one 15 ml spoon
1 teaspoon = one 5 ml spoon.

Use fresh herbs and freshly ground black pepper unless otherwise stated.

Use standard size 3 eggs unless otherwise suggested.

CONTENTS

INTRODUCTION

Stir frying is the cooking technique we normally associate with Chinese cooking. Small pieces of food are quickly fried over a high heat until just tender. The foods are cut to a similar size and are added to the pan in stages; those requiring the longest cooking time are added first with the delicate, quick-cooking pieces added at the end.

When time is at a premium, the technique of stir frying is the perfect choice. Cooking times are invariably brief and it's possible to cook a complete meal in one pan. It therefore seems to me a shame to confine this method of cooking to Chinese dishes. Vegetables, lean meat, fish and seafood, even fruits, can all be stir fried with a variety of flavourings to produce all manner of enticing dishes. Stir frying is a healthy way of cooking, too. Only a small amount of oil or fat need be used and quick cooking ensures foods retain their nutrients as well as flavour.

The best sort of pan to use is obviously a wok. Its large proportions and rounded shape are perfect for stir frying. I find the easiest type to use is one with a single handle and, for ease of cleaning, I'd choose a modern non-stick one. If you prefer a traditional wok, you should be able to buy one quite cheaply from a Chinese supermarket. It will perform well but, unless it's in constant use, you will need to be meticulous about cleaning and oiling to prevent it from rusting.

If you cook on an electric cooker with radiant or solid rings or a ceramic hob, rather than gas burners, then a flat bottomed wok is really a must. The cooking temperature will not be high enough if you use a rounded wok perched above the heat on a trivet. A large deep sided frying pan or a sauté pan with a lid can be used instead of a wok for most of the recipes in this book.

Always make sure the oil is really hot before you add the ingredients to the wok or pan. Stir them constantly and vigorously during the brief cooking time, using a long handled wooden spoon to ensure the food is evenly cooked. Avoid overcooking at all costs or you will lose texture and colour. Stir fried dishes are at their best served immediately.

The collection of stir fry recipes in this book includes vegetables, salads, fish, meat, rice dishes, noodles and desserts. They are not all oriental in nature, because – in devising these recipes – I have attempted to show you just how versatile, quick and easy stir fries can be. I hope you will enjoy trying out the recipes on your family and friends, and use them to develop your own ideas.

SALADS

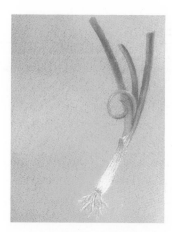

Salads are no longer entirely cold affairs. In cafés, brasseries and restaurants there is a trend towards combining hot dressings with leafy mixtures; hot cooked foods with raw. Stir frying is the ideal way to prepare instant hot tasty dressings.

In this chapter I have included recipes for modern day 'classics' such as brandied chicken livers with salad leaves, and gado gado, as well as some of my own favourite combinations, such as salami and omelette salad. Serve these 'hot' salads as starters, or light meals with crusty bread.

CONTENTS

CHICKEN LIVERS WITH SALAD LEAVES

SERVES 3-4

This quantity is sufficient to serve four as a starter or three as a light main course accompanied by crusty bread or toast.

about 250 g (8 oz) mixed salad leaves, e.g. frisée (curly endive), chicory and lamb's lettuce
25 g (1 oz) unsalted butter
3 tablespoons olive or groundnut oil
500 g (1 lb) chicken livers, halved
1 small red onion, quartered and separated into petals
1 tablespoon red wine vinegar
1 teaspoon Dijon mustard
4 tablespoons brandy
1 teaspoon chopped thyme
salt and pepper to taste

TO GARNISH
thyme sprigs

1. Arrange the mixed salad leaves on individual serving plates.

2. Heat the butter and oil in a large frying pan or wok. Add the chicken livers and stir fry over a high heat for 2 minutes to seal. Add the onion and continue stir frying for 2 minutes until the chicken livers are browned on the outside but still pink and tender within.

3. Add the vinegar, mustard, brandy and thyme and toss gently over the heat to mix. Add seasoning.

4. Spoon the chicken mixture and juices on top of the salad leaves and serve at once, garnished with thyme sprigs.

BACON WRAPPED PRAWN SALAD

SERVES 4

This is a wonderful summer lunch. I also make a simplified version – omitting the cooked vegetables – to serve as a starter.

½ head oakleaf lettuce
about 75 g (3 oz) rocket
175 g (6 oz) red or yellow cherry tomatoes, halved
6 rashers streaky bacon, rinds removed
12 cooked King prawns, peeled and deveined
3 tablespoons olive oil
250 g (8 oz) mangetout
½ red or yellow pepper, cored, seeded and cut into thin strips
2 tablespoons walnut or hazelnut oil
2 tablespoons tarragon or wine vinegar
grated rind and juice of ½ lemon
pepper to taste

1. Tear the salad leaves into bite-sized pieces and arrange on individual serving plates with the cherry tomatoes.

2. Cut each bacon rasher in half and stretch, using the back of a knife. Wrap a half rasher around each prawn.

3. Heat the olive oil in a wok or large frying pan. Add the bacon-wrapped prawns and stir fry over a fairly high heat for 3 minutes. Add the mangetout and pepper strips and stir fry for 2 minutes.

4. Add the nut oil, vinegar, lemon rind and juice. Toss gently and season with pepper. Spoon over the salad and serve at once.

ABOVE: CHICKEN LIVERS WITH SALAD LEAVES *BELOW*: BACON-WRAPPED PRAWN SALAD

HOT BACON & PECAN SALAD

SERVES 4

Chicory is one of my favourite 'hot' salad ingredients. The firm texture is retained, while its bitter flavour is pleasantly tempered by the heat of the dressing.

2 heads chicory
½ head frisée (curly endive)
1 bunch watercress
1 orange, peeled and segmented
½ onion, thinly sliced
4 tablespoons olive oil
250 g (8 oz) bacon rashers, derinded and
  chopped
1 clove garlic, crushed
50 g (2 oz) pecans
3 tablespoons freshly squeezed orange juice
2 tablespoons sherry vinegar
1 teaspoon Dijon mustard
salt and pepper to taste

1. Arrange the chicory, frisée (endive), watercress, orange and onion on individual plates.

2. Heat 2 tablespoons oil in a large frying pan or wok. Add the bacon and stir fry for 2 minutes. Stir in the garlic and pecans and cook for 1 minute.

3. Add the remaining oil to the pan together with the orange juice, vinegar, mustard and seasoning. Stir well.

4. Spoon the hot dressing over the salad and serve at once.

SALAMI & OMELETTE SALAD

SERVES 4

2 eggs
15 g (½ oz) butter
1 cos lettuce, roughly torn
75 g (3 oz) salami, finely sliced
handful of black olives
4 tablespoons olive oil
½ red pepper, cored, seeded and cut into thin
  strips
2 tablespoons capers
2 tablespoons wine vinegar
½ teaspoon Dijon mustard
pinch of sugar
salt and pepper to taste

1. Lightly beat the eggs with 2 tablespoons water. Melt the butter in a large non-stick frying pan and add the beaten egg. Cook over a medium heat, using a spatula to push the cooked edges into the centre and tilting the pan, until the omelette is softly set. Transfer to a plate, roll up and allow to cool. Slice the omelette and arrange on a serving plate with the lettuce, salami and olives.

2. Add the olive oil to the pan and return to the heat. Add the pepper strips and stir fry for 1 minute. Stir in the remaining ingredients.

3. Spoon the hot dressing over the salad to serve.

GADO GADO

SERVES 4-6

A protein-packed Indonesian salad, combining crisply cooked and raw vegetables, ribbons of omelette and a spicy peanut sauce. Vary the vegetables as you like – to include baby corn cobs, leeks, French beans or cauliflower if you prefer.

2 eggs
3 tablespoons groundnut oil
250 g (8 oz) carrot
3 celery sticks
1 clove garlic, halved
125 g (4 oz) mangetout
½ head Chinese leaf, shredded
175 g (6 oz) bean sprouts
125 g (4 oz) radishes, sliced

PEANUT SAUCE
25 g (1 oz) creamed coconut
6 tablespoons milk
¼ onion, chopped
1 clove garlic, crushed
4 tablespoons peanut butter
½ teaspoon ground cumin
½ teaspoon chilli powder
1 tablespoon soy sauce
pinch of sugar

1 First make the peanut sauce: chop the creamed coconut and place in a blender or food processor with the milk. Blend to a paste. Add all the remaining ingredients and purée until smooth.

2 To prepare the omelette, lightly beat the eggs with 2 tablespoons water. Heat 1 tablespoon of the oil in a large non-stick frying pan and add the beaten egg. Cook over a medium heat using a spatula to push the cooked edges into the centre and tilting the pan as the omelette cooks. When the omelette is golden brown underneath, turn to cook the underside. Remove from the pan and set aside.

3 Cut the carrot and celery into julienne (matchstick strips). Heat the remaining oil in the same pan or wok. Add the garlic, carrot, celery and mangetout and stir fry for 2-3 minutes until just tender. Transfer to a salad bowl, discarding the garlic, and allow to cool.

4 Cut the prepared omelette into thin ribbons and add to the salad bowl with the Chinese leaf, bean sprouts and radishes. Toss gently to mix.

5 Spoon the peanut sauce over the salad to serve.

Note This looks most attractive garnished with radish roses. Simply make crosswise cuts through the radish from the top almost through to the base and leave in a bowl of iced water for about 20 minutes to open out.

MANGO, CHICKEN & SPINACH SALAD

SERVES 4

Serve this delicious combination as a substantial starter or light meal.

1 large ripe mango
3 skinless chicken breast fillets
175 g (6 oz) young spinach leaves
1 teaspoon sesame oil
5 tablespoons groundnut or olive oil
1 clove garlic, crushed
3 spring onions, sliced
2 tablespoons sherry vinegar
1/2 teaspoon soft dark brown sugar
50 g (2 oz) salted cashew nuts
handful of coriander leaves
salt and pepper to taste

1 Peel the mango and slice thinly, discarding the stone. Cut the chicken crosswise into strips.

2 Tear the spinach into bite-size pieces and arrange on individual plates.

3 Heat the sesame oil and 3 tablespoons groundnut or olive oil in a wok. Add the chicken and stir fry over a high heat for 2 minutes. Add the garlic and continue stir frying for 1 minute. Stir in the spring onions and cook for a few seconds.

4 Add the remaining oil to the wok with the vinegar and sugar. Stir in the mango, cashews, coriander and seasoning; heat through.

5 Spoon the chicken mixture on top of the spinach leaves and serve at once.

CHEESE SALAD WITH MIXED HOT NUTS

SERVES 4

A lightly dressed salad with garlic and herb cheese and hot, spicy nuts. Use other kinds of nuts if you prefer, such as walnuts, pecans and hazelnuts.

1 head lollo rosso, roughly torn
50 g (2 oz) rocket
handful of chervil sprigs, roughly torn
2 celery sticks, chopped
1 red apple, cored and sliced
142 g (5 oz) Boursin with garlic and herbs

DRESSING
2 tablespoons olive oil
1 tablespoon red wine vinegar
pinch of sugar
salt and pepper to taste

MIXED NUTS
50 g (2 oz) blanched almonds
50 g (2 oz) peanuts or cashews
25 g (1 oz) pine nuts
25 g (1 oz) butter
1/2 teaspoon paprika
1/2 teaspoon mild chilli powder
pinch of ground cumin
sea salt to taste

1 Put the salad leaves and chervil in a bowl with the celery and apple.

2 Mix together the dressing ingredients, add to the salad and toss gently to coat. Crumble the soft cheese over the top.

3 Stir fry the nuts in a frying pan over medium heat for 4-5 minutes to brown. Add the butter and stir fry for 1 minute until sizzling. Stir in the spices and salt. Let cool for 1 minute. Sprinkle over salad and serve.

FISH & SHELLFISH

Quick cooking fish and seafood is perfect for stir frying; even large hearty pieces need only a short cooking time. Choose fish that is firm and succulent for these dishes, so that it does not break up on stirring.

For a tasty fish supper that can be on the table in less than 10 minutes try stir fried fish with tomato and herbs, or lemon sole with lettuce. If you are entertaining, tempt your guests with scallops in saffron cream sauce, or Caledonian salmon with gingered vegetables.

CONTENTS

QUICK FRIED PRAWNS WITH GINGER

SERVES 3-4

Sample these truly delicious mouthfuls of prawns with garlic, ginger and spring onion – quick fried in a light sherry batter. Serve as a starter or with rice as part of an oriental meal.

---

12 raw King prawns
1 teaspoon grated fresh root ginger
½ clove garlic, crushed
2 spring onions, very finely chopped
3 tablespoons self-raising flour
salt and pepper to taste
2 teaspoons sherry
1 egg, beaten
about 175 ml (6 fl oz) groundnut oil for frying
lemon wedges to garnish

1 Peel and devein the prawns, leaving the tail shells on. Place in a bowl with the ginger, garlic and spring onions; mix well.

2 Put the flour in a bowl, season and add the sherry and egg. Beat to a smooth batter. Fold in the prawns and toss to coat.

3 Heat the oil in a wok until very hot. Fry the prawns, in batches, for 2-3 minutes until golden brown and cook through. Drain on kitchen paper and keep hot while cooking the rest.

4 Transfer to a warmed serving dish and serve at once, garnished with lemon wedges.

MUSSELS IN BLACK BEAN SAUCE

SERVES 2-4

I love to eat this as a starter, scooping up the rich salty black bean sauce with the mussel shells. You can of course serve it as a main course, with rice.

---

750 g (1½ lb) fresh mussels
4 tablespoons sherry
2 tablespoons groundnut oil
1 clove garlic, crushed
2.5 cm (1 inch) piece fresh root ginger, grated
3 spring onions, chopped
1 teaspoon cornflour
2 tablespoons light soy sauce
½ teaspoon sugar
50 g (2 oz) canned black beans, rinsed
pepper to taste

1 Scrub the mussels thoroughly in cold water, removing their beards. Discard any with open or damaged shells.

2 Put 125 ml (4 fl oz) water in a wok or sauté pan with 2 tablespoons of the sherry and bring to the boil. Add the mussels, cover and cook for 2-3 minutes, shaking the pan once or twice, until the shells have opened. Discard any unopened mussels. Strain, reserving 6 tablespoons liquid.

3 Heat the oil in the dry wok. Add the garlic, ginger and spring onions and stir fry for 1 minute.

4 Blend the cornflour with the soy sauce, remaining sherry, sugar and mussel liquid. Add to the wok with the black beans and stir until thickened. Return the mussels to the pan and heat through, stirring. Season and serve immediately.

ABOVE: MUSSELS IN BLACK BEAN SAUCE *BELOW*: QUICK FRIED PRAWNS WITH GINGER

PRAWN KORMA

SERVES 4

Prawns don't need a lengthy cooking time so stir frying is the perfect way to cook this mild Indian curry. Buy creamed coconut in blocks from supermarkets or ethnic stores.

25 g (1 oz) butter
2 tablespoons oil
2 onions, cut into wedges
250 g (8 oz) potato, diced
1-2 cloves garlic, crushed
2.5 cm (1 inch) piece fresh root ginger, grated
1 chilli, seeded and chopped
2 teaspoons ground coriander
1 teaspoon ground cumin
1½ teaspoons turmeric
½ teaspoon allspice
25 g (1 oz) creamed coconut, chopped
300 ml (½ pint) light stock or water
12 cooked King prawns
75 g (3 oz) frozen peas, thawed
1 tablespoon roughly chopped coriander leaves
2 tablespoons cream or thick yogurt

TO GARNISH
coriander leaves

1 Heat the butter and oil in a large shallow pan or wok. Add the onions, potato and garlic and stir fry for 5 minutes to soften. Stir in the ginger, chilli and spices and fry gently for a further 4 minutes.

2 Add the creamed coconut and stock or water to the pan. Bring to the boil and simmer for 5 minutes. Stir in the prawns, peas and coriander. Cover and cook for 2-3 minutes.

3 Stir in the cream or yogurt and seasoning. Serve hot, garnished with coriander and accompanied by basmati rice.

MONKFISH WITH OKRA & TOMATO

SERVES 4

625 g (1¼ lb) monkfish fillet
250 g (8 oz) okra
4 tablespoons wine vinegar
3 tablespoons virgin olive oil
3 rashers smoked bacon, derinded and chopped
1 onion, chopped
1-2 cloves garlic, crushed
500 g (1 lb) tomatoes, skinned and cut into wedges
3 basil sprigs
1 thyme sprig
200 ml (7 fl oz) dry white wine
2 tablespoons chopped parsley
salt and pepper to taste

TO GARNISH
herb sprigs

1 Cut the fish into 2.5 cm (1 inch) slices.

2 Cut the okra diagonally into thick slices. Place in a bowl and add water to cover. Add the vinegar and leave to stand for 10 minutes then rinse thoroughly and pat dry.

3 Heat the oil in a wok or large sauté pan with a lid. Add the bacon, onion and garlic and stir fry over a medium heat for 3 minutes to soften. Stir in the tomatoes, basil, thyme and wine and cook for 2 minutes.

4 Add the okra and monkfish to the pan, together with the parsley and seasoning. Cover and cook for about 4 minutes until the monkfish is firm and opaque and the okra is just tender. Serve immediately, garnished with herbs.

LEMON SOLE & LETTUCE

SERVES 4-6

Stir fried strips of sole fillet in a light lemon sauce are served on a bed of cucumber and lettuce. Accompany this tasty dish with rice or noodles.

1 egg white
1 tablespoon cornflour
1 tablespoon light soy sauce
½ teaspoon Chinese five-spice powder
salt and pepper to taste
500 g (1 lb) sole fillets, skinned
4 tablespoons groundnut oil
1 clove garlic, crushed
2.5 cm (1 inch) piece fresh root ginger, thinly sliced
4 spring onions, cut into 5 cm (2 inch) lengths
½ cucumber, halved lengthways, seeded and sliced
½ cos lettuce, shredded

SAUCE
juice of 2 lemons
½ teaspoon finely grated lemon rind
6 tablespoons water
2 tablespoons sherry
2 tablespoons soy sauce
1 tablespoon wine vinegar
2 tablespoons sugar
1 tablespoon cornflour

TO GARNISH
lemon slices and chives

1. Mix together all the ingredients for the sauce in a bowl and set aside.

2. In another bowl, whisk the egg white until frothy, then stir in the cornflour, soy sauce, five-spice powder and seasoning.

3. Cut the sole fillets into wide strips, add to the egg mixture and toss to coat.

4. Heat the oil in a wok. Fry fish in batches for 1 minute only on each side. Drain on kitchen paper, transfer to a warmed serving plate and keep warm.

5. Pour off all but 2 tablespoons oil from the wok. Add the garlic, ginger and spring onions and stir fry for 1 minute. Pour in the sauce mixture and stir until thickened.

6. Stir in the cucumber and lettuce and cook for 1-2 minutes. Adjust the seasoning.

7. Spoon the vegetables and lemon sauce over the fish and serve at once, garnished with lemon slices and chives.

FISH WITH LEEKS & RED PEPPER

SERVES 4

If you cannot get fresh small venus clams, use a jar of clams instead. Serve this tasty dish with plenty of crusty bread for mopping up the juices.

3 tablespoons olive oil
1 clove garlic, crushed
1 celery stick, chopped
2 leeks, sliced
1 red pepper, cored, seeded and sliced
400 g (14 oz) can chopped tomatoes
150 ml (¼ pint) white wine
1 tablespoon chopped parsley
500 g (1 lb) cod or haddock fillet, skinned and
    diced
250 g (8 oz) mackerel fillet, diced
350 g (12 oz) clams, scrubbed
salt and pepper to taste

1 Heat the oil in a large shallow pan or wok. Add the garlic, celery, leeks and red pepper and stir fry for 3 minutes.

2 Stir in the tomatoes, white wine and 150 ml (¼ pint) water. Bring to the boil, then lower the heat and simmer for 3 minutes. Stir in the parsley, fish and clams and cook gently for about 5 minutes until the clams are open and the fish is opaque and cooked through. Season and serve immediately.

SEAFOOD WITH FENNEL & TOMATOES

SERVES 4

A delicious combination of stir fried fennel, onion and garlic with a medley of seafood.

6 tablespoons virgin olive oil
2 onions, chopped
1 small fennel bulb, sliced
2 cloves garlic, crushed
4 large tomatoes, peeled and chopped
bouquet garni
1 bay leaf
large strip of lemon peel
large pinch of powdered saffron
500 g (1 lb) mixed fish fillet, skinned and cut into
    bite-size pieces, e.g. monkfish, conger eel, red
    mullet, snapper
250 g (8 oz) raw King prawns, peeled and
    deveined
salt and pepper to taste

TO GARNISH
snipped chives

1 Heat 3 tablespoons of the oil in a wok or sauté pan. Add the onions, fennel and garlic and stir fry over a gentle heat, for 8 minutes.

2 Add the tomatoes, bouquet garni, bay leaf, lemon peel and saffron, with the remaining oil and 150 ml (¼ pint) boiling water. Bring to a rapid boil, then lower the heat.

3 Add the fish in stages; firmer fish such as monkfish and conger eel first, followed by the more flaky varieties such as mullet and snapper; finally add the prawns. Simmer for 5 minutes, until just cooked.

4 Season to taste and garnish with snipped chives.

ABOVE: SEAFOOD WITH FENNEL & TOMATOES BELOW: FISH WITH LEEKS & RED PEPPER

STIR FRIED FISH WITH TOMATO & HERBS

SERVES 4

Choose firm white fish for this recipe, such as cod, haddock or monkfish, and select herbs according to preference. Serve with plain boiled rice.

3 tablespoons virgin olive oil
1 clove garlic, crushed
2 celery sticks, cut into julienne strips
3 spring onions, diagonally sliced
125 ml (4 fl oz) dry white wine
2 teaspoons tomato purée
pinch of sugar
500 g (1 lb) white fish fillet, skinned and cut into
*   chunks*
125 g (4 oz) mangetout
3 tomatoes, skinned and cut into wedges
2 tablespoons chopped herbs, e.g. coriander, basil,
*   parsley, chives*
salt and pepper to taste

TO GARNISH
herb sprigs

1 Heat the oil in a large frying pan or wok. Add the garlic, celery and spring onions and stir fry for 1 minute. Stir in the dry white wine, tomato purée and sugar.

2 Add the fish to the pan, cover and cook for 2-3 minutes.

3 Gently stir in the mangetout, tomatoes and herbs. Cook for 1-2 minutes until the fish is firm and the mangetout are just tender. Season and serve garnished with herb sprigs.

SCALLOPS IN SAFFRON CREAM SAUCE

SERVES 4

Succulent plump scallops are stir fried with celery and carrot and served in a wine and cream sauce flavoured with saffron. Serve with rice – preferably a mixture of white and wild rice.

pinch of saffron threads
25 g (1 oz) butter
1 shallot, finely chopped
3 celery sticks, cut into julienne strips
2 carrots, cut into julienne strips
12 large scallops
125 ml (4 fl oz) dry white wine
4 tablespoons double cream
salt and pepper to taste

TO GARNISH
chervil

1 Place the saffron threads in a cup and add 125 ml (4 fl oz) boiling water. Leave to infuse for 15 minutes.

2 Heat the butter in a large frying pan or wok. Add the shallot, celery and carrots and stir fry for 1 minute. Add the scallops and stir fry for 1 minute.

3 Stir in the wine and saffron with its liquid. Bring to the boil, cover and allow to simmer for 4-5 minutes until the scallops are just firm and cooked. Stir in the cream and seasoning and heat through gently.

4 Serve immediately, sprinkled with chervil.

CALEDONIAN SALMON WITH GINGERED VEGETABLES

SERVES 4

Fresh salmon fillet steamed over a bed of stir fried vegetables and slivers of ginger is a perfectly simple yet delicious special occasion main course. Caledonian fillets are thick slices of salmon fillet – boneless and skinned – which are available from large supermarkets. Alternatively, you can use salmon steaks for this recipe but you will need a pan large enough to take 4 steaks in one layer, and to increase the cooking time by a minute or two.

6 tablespoons groundnut oil
2 teaspoons sesame oil
1/2 clove garlic, crushed
5 cm (2 inch) piece fresh root ginger, thinly sliced
pinch of Chinese five-spice powder
350 g (12 oz) small baby carrots, halved
   lengthwise
1 fennel bulb, cut into strips
1 courgette, cut into strips
3 spring onions, sliced
227 g (8 oz) can bamboo shoots, drained and
   sliced
2 tablespoons light soy sauce
pinch of sugar
1 tablespoon chopped coriander leaves
4 Caledonian salmon fillets, each about 175 g
   (6 oz)
salt and pepper to taste
4 tablespoons sherry

1 Heat the oils in a large frying pan or wok. Add the garlic, ginger, five-spice powder, carrots, fennel, courgette, spring onions and bamboo shoots and stir fry for 1 minute. Stir in the soy sauce, sugar and coriander.

2 Arrange the salmon in one layer on top of the vegetables, season with salt and pepper and spoon over the sherry. Cover with a tight fitting lid and cook over a medium heat for 7-8 minutes until the fish is opaque and cooked; do not overcook.

3 Carefully transfer the salmon to warmed serving plates and surround with the vegetables. Spoon the juices over and serve at once, accompanied by crusty bread.

RIGHT: CALEDONIAN SALMON WITH GINGERED VEGETABLES

COD WITH BROCCOLI & RED PEPPER

SERVES 3-4

Quick fried pieces of cod with broccoli, red onion and pepper in black bean sauce. Use canned rather than dried beans and rinse well as they are salty.

1 egg white
4 teaspoons cornflour
2 tablespoons soy sauce
500 g (1 lb) cod fillet, skinned and cubed
150 ml (¼ pint) groundnut oil
1 clove garlic, crushed
2.5 cm (1 inch) piece fresh root ginger, grated
1 small red onion, cut into wedges
175 g (6 oz) broccoli florets
1 red pepper, cored, seeded and cut into strips
3 tablespoons sherry
2 tablespoons oyster sauce
2 tablespoons canned black beans, rinsed
pepper to taste

1 Whisk the egg white until frothy and stir in 3 teaspoons cornflour and 1 tablespoon soy sauce. Add the fish and mix well.

2 Heat the oil in a wok. Fry the fish, in batches, for about 2 minutes until cooked through. Drain on kitchen paper; set aside.

3 Pour off all but 3 tablespoons oil from the wok. Add the garlic, ginger, onion, broccoli and red pepper and stir fry for 3 minutes.

4 Mix together the remaining cornflour, soy sauce, sherry, oyster sauce and 2 tablespoons water. Add to the wok with the black beans and pepper; stir until thickened.

5 Return the fish to the wok and heat through, stirring gently. Serve at once.

SWEET & SOUR FISH BALLS

SERVES 4

Serve this tasty stir fry with simple egg fried rice, or herb and sesame noodles.

3 tablespoons groundnut oil
1 clove garlic, crushed
125 g (4 oz) mangetout
1 carrot, diagonally sliced
125 g (4 oz) baby corn cobs, halved lengthwise
2 spring onions, sliced
227 g (8 oz) can pineapple pieces in juice
125 ml (4 fl oz) chicken or fish stock
2 tablespoons sherry
3 tablespoons wine vinegar
2 tablespoons light soy sauce
1 tablespoon cornflour
1 tablespoon sugar

FISH BALLS
350 g (12 oz) cod fillet, skinned and diced
125 g (4 oz) peeled prawns
2 spring onions, chopped
1 tablespoon sherry
1 tablespoon light soy sauce
1 egg white
salt and pepper to taste

1 Put all the ingredients for the fish balls in a food processor or blender and process until almost smooth. With dampened hands, shape the mixture into 16 balls.

2 Heat the oil in a wok. Add the garlic and vegetables and stir fry for 2 minutes. Add the pineapple, reserving the juice.

3 Blend the pineapple juice with the remaining ingredients and add to the wok. Stir until thickened. Add the fish balls, cover and cook gently for 4-5 minutes until the fish is opaque and cooked.

ABOVE: SWEET & SOUR FISH BALLS *BELOW*: COD WITH BROCCOLI & RED PEPPER

SIZZLING TROUT WITH GARLIC & SPRING ONIONS

SERVES 2

For a fast lunch or supper try this simply delicious pan-fried trout with garlic, spring onions, parsley and a hint of ginger and lemon. Serve with new potatoes and a salad.

2 trout, cleaned
25 g (1 oz) butter
2 tablespoons virgin olive oil
2 cloves garlic, thinly sliced
½ teaspoon grated fresh root ginger
4 spring onions, sliced
1 tablespoon chopped parsley
juice of ½ lemon
¼ teaspoon finely grated lemon rind
salt and pepper to taste

TO GARNISH
lemon wedges

1 Wash the trout and remove the heads. Using a sharp knife, make 2 or 3 slashes through the skin on each side of the fish.

2 Heat 15 g (½ oz) of the butter and 1 tablespoon oil in a large frying pan. Add the trout and fry for about 4 minutes on each side until just cooked. Transfer to a plate and keep hot.

3 Add the rest of the butter and oil to the pan. Add the garlic, ginger and spring onions and stir fry for 1 minute, then stir in the remaining ingredients and return the trout to the pan. Cook for 1 minute over a high heat until hot and sizzling. Serve at once, garnished with lemon wedges.

SMOKED HADDOCK WITH SPRING VEGETABLES

SERVES 4

Serve this tasty dish of smoked haddock, young carrots and courgettes in a herb and cream sauce with rice or pasta.

25 g (1 oz) butter
250 g (8 oz) small baby carrots, halved lengthwise
2 small courgettes, cut into julienne strips
4 spring onions, cut into 5 cm (2 inch) lengths
juice of ½ lemon
500 g (1 lb) smoked haddock fillet, skinned and diced
300 ml (½ pint) milk
1 teaspoon chopped parsley
1 teaspoon chopped tarragon
4 tablespoons double cream
pepper to taste

TO GARNISH
tarragon sprigs

1 Heat the butter in a large shallow pan or wok. Add the vegetables and stir fry for 2 minutes. Add the lemon juice and smoked haddock and stir fry for 2 minutes, taking care not to break up the fish.

2 Add the milk to the pan and bring to the boil. Lower the heat and simmer for 4-5 minutes until the fish is cooked.

3 Gently stir in the parsley, tarragon, cream and seasoning. Serve, garnished with tarragon.

ABOVE: SIZZLING TROUT WITH GARLIC & SPRING ONIONS BELOW: SMOKED HADDOCK WITH SPRING VEGETABLES

MEAT DISHES

Stir frying is a good way of making the most of the finer cuts of meat. It is true that only tender cuts of meat are suitable for stir fry recipes but a little goes a long way. Choose cuts of meat such as lean fillet, rump steak and lean boneless chops.

If you have time, allow the meat to marinate in the sherry, soy sauce, garlic and ginger for a short while before cooking. As with all foods for stir frying, cut meat into equal size pieces for even cooking.

CONTENTS

LEMON CHICKEN

SERVES 4

I find the lemon sauce pleasantly sharp with just 1 teaspoon honey, but you may prefer to add more.

4 skinless chicken breast fillets
1 egg white
1 tablespoon light soy sauce
1 tablespoon sherry
1 tablespoon cornflour
salt and pepper to taste
3 tablespoons groundnut oil
1 teaspoon sesame oil
1 clove garlic, crushed
2.5 cm (1 inch) piece fresh root ginger, chopped
3 spring onions, diagonally sliced
½ lemon, thinly sliced

SAUCE
2 teaspoons cornflour
1-2 teaspoons clear honey
2 tablespoons light soy sauce
300 ml (½ pint) chicken stock
shredded finely pared rind of 1 lemon

1 Mix together the sauce ingredients; set aside.

2 Thickly slice the chicken, then place between 2 sheets of greaseproof paper and beat with a rolling pin to flatten. Whisk together the egg white, soy sauce, sherry, cornflour and seasoning. Add the chicken and mix well.

3 Heat the oils in a wok and stir fry the chicken for 3 minutes, or until just cooked. Transfer to a serving plate; keep hot.

4 Add the garlic and ginger to the wok. Stir fry for 2 minutes. Pour in the sauce and cook, stirring, until thickened. Add the spring onions and lemon slices and cook for 1 minute. Pour over the chicken.

CHICKEN WITH BROCCOLI & GINGER

SERVES 4

Serve with egg fried rice or noodles for a simple meal. You could replace the chicken with slivers of beef or pork.

3 tablespoons groundnut oil
few drops of sesame oil
500 g (1 lb) skinless chicken breast fillets, sliced
2.5 cm (1 inch) piece fresh root ginger, grated
1 clove garlic, crushed
1 small red pepper, cored, seeded and thinly sliced
250 g (8 oz) broccoli, in small florets
4 spring onions, sliced
50 g (2 oz) salted cashew nuts
Szechuan or black pepper to taste

SAUCE
2 tablespoons dark soy sauce
4 tablespoons sherry
150 ml (¼ pint) water
1 tablespoon cornflour

1 Mix the sauce ingredients together in a small bowl and set aside.

2 Heat the oils in a wok, add the chicken and stir fry for 2 minutes. Add the ginger, garlic, red pepper and broccoli and stir fry for 3 minutes.

3 Pour in the sauce and stir fry for 2-3 minutes until thickened and the chicken and vegetables are cooked. Stir in the spring onions and cashew nuts and cook for a few seconds. Add seasoning and serve at once.

CHICKEN WITH GOLDEN VEGETABLES

SERVES 4

Sweet pumpkin flesh is delicious stir-fried. Here it is combined with carrot, baby corn and chicken in a warming, golden dish.

500 g (1 lb) skinless chicken breast fillets
3-4 tablespoons groundnut oil
few drops of sesame oil
1 clove garlic, crushed
2.5 cm (1 inch) piece fresh root ginger, grated
350 g (12 oz) pumpkin, cut into strips
1 large carrot, cut into strips
125 g (4 oz) baby corn cobs, halved lengthwise
4 spring onions, sliced diagonally
2 tablespoons dark soy sauce
2 tablespoons light soy sauce
3 tablespoons sherry
2-3 tablespoons yellow bean paste
pepper to taste

1 Cut the chicken into finger-sized slices. Heat the oils in a wok, add the chicken and stir fry for 3 minutes. Transfer to a plate, using a slotted spoon.

2 Add the garlic, ginger and pumpkin to the wok, with a little more oil if necessary. Stir fry for 5 minutes.

3 Add the carrot, baby corn and spring onions and stir fry for 5 minutes, then stir in the soy sauce, sherry and yellow bean paste. Return the chicken to the wok, season with pepper and cook for 3-4 minutes until the chicken and vegetables are tender. Serve immediately.

CHICKEN STIR FRY WITH NOODLES

SERVES 4

3 skinless chicken breast fillets, cut into strips
250 g (8 oz) chicken livers, halved
3 tablespoons Worcestershire sauce
2 tablespoons soy sauce
175 g (6 oz) rice ribbon noodles
1 teaspoon sesame oil
2 tablespoons groundnut oil
1 clove garlic, crushed
2.5 cm (1 inch) piece fresh root ginger, grated
1 small onion, cut into wedges
175 g (6 oz) broccoli florets
1 teaspoon cornflour
2 tablespoons sherry
2 tomatoes, skinned and cut into wedges
salt and pepper to taste
1 teaspoon toasted sesame seeds

1 Place the chicken and livers in a bowl. Add the Worcestershire and soy sauces and mix well. Leave to marinate for 20 minutes.

2 Cook the noodles according to packet instructions. Drain, toss in the sesame oil and keep hot in a warmed serving dish.

3 Meanwhile, heat the groundnut oil in a wok. Using a slotted spoon, add the chicken and livers, with the garlic, and stir fry for 2 minutes. Add the ginger, onion and broccoli and stir fry for 2 minutes.

4 Blend the cornflour with the sherry, remaining marinade and 2 tablespoons water. Add to the wok and stir until thickened. Add the tomatoes and seasoning and cook for 1 minute.

5 Spoon over the noodles and serve at once, sprinkled with toasted sesame seeds.

CHICKEN WITH REDCURRANTS

SERVES 4

Serve this with rice or a simple noodle dish, such as herb and sesame noodles.

4 chicken quarters, skinned
2 tablespoons light soy sauce
3 tablespoons groundnut oil
few drops of sesame oil
1 clove garlic, thinly sliced
2.5 cm (1 inch) piece fresh root ginger, shredded
1 red onion, cut into thin wedges
4 tablespoons redcurrant jelly
juice of 1 lemon
4 tablespoons chicken stock
50 g (2 oz) redcurrants (fresh or frozen)
salt and pepper to taste
1 tablespoon snipped chives

TO GARNISH
redcurrant sprigs and chives

1. Rub the chicken with the soy sauce and leave for 10 minutes.

2. Heat the oils in a wok or large sauté pan. Add the chicken and cook for 2-3 minutes, turning until browned all over. Remove and set aside.

3. Add the garlic, ginger and onion to the pan and stir fry for 2 minutes. Stir in the redcurrant jelly, lemon juice and stock.

4. Return the chicken to the pan, cover and simmer for 15-20 minutes, until tender, then uncover and boil rapidly to reduce the liquid.

5. Stir in the redcurrants and seasoning and cook for 1 minute. Serve, sprinkled with snipped chives. Garnish with redcurrant sprigs and chives.

DUCK WITH CALVADOS & APPLES

SERVES 4

2 tablespoons light olive oil
500 g (1 lb) boneless duck breasts, skinned and cut into strips
salt and pepper to taste
50 g (2 oz) butter
1 shallot, chopped
1 clove garlic, chopped
2 rashers streaky bacon, derinded and chopped
175 g (6 oz) whole open cup mushrooms
6 tablespoons Calvados or brandy
2 teaspoons finely chopped thyme
3 tablespoons double cream
2 dessert apples, peeled, cored and cut into thick wedges

TO GARNISH
thyme sprigs

1. Heat the oil in a wok or large sauté pan. Add the duck and stir fry for 3 minutes. Season, then remove and set aside.

2. Add half the butter to the pan and heat gently. Add the shallot, garlic, bacon and mushrooms and stir fry for 3 minutes.

3. Return the duck to the pan and add the Calvados or brandy and thyme. Cook over a fairly high heat for about 2 minutes to reduce the juices, then lower the heat and stir in the cream. Adjust the seasoning and transfer to a warmed serving plate; keep hot.

4. To prepare the apples, melt the remaining butter in a clean pan and quickly fry the apple wedges until golden brown. Arrange around the duck and garnish with thyme to serve.

ABOVE: DUCK WITH CALVADOS & APPLES *BELOW*: CHICKEN WITH REDCURRANTS

PORK FILLET WITH BABY CORN

SERVES 4

Tenderloin of pork is superb for stir fry recipes. It is easily sliced into thin, even pieces and is so tender it needs only the shortest cooking time. Serve this dish with rice, noodles or new potatoes, and a green vegetable or leafy salad.

500 g (1 lb) pork fillet (tenderloin)
1½ tablespoons green peppercorns in brine, drained
3 tablespoons groundnut oil
1 shallot, finely chopped
1 clove garlic, crushed
175 g (6 oz) baby corn cobs, halved lengthwise
2 tablespoons brandy or dry vermouth
4 tablespoons double cream
salt to taste

TO GARNISH
mint sprigs

1 Cut the pork into thin slices. Lightly crush the green peppercorns using a pestle and mortar or rolling pin. Set aside.

2 Heat the oil in a wok or large frying pan. Add the pork and stir fry over a high heat for 1 minute. Add the shallot and garlic and continue stir frying for 2 minutes.

3 Add the corn cobs to the wok and stir fry for 1-2 minutes until they are almost tender. Stir in the crushed peppercorns, brandy or vermouth. Cook over a high heat until the juices are reduced to about 1 tablespoon. Lower the heat and stir in the cream. Season with salt and serve immediately, garnished with mint sprigs.

PORK WITH WATER CHESTNUTS

SERVES 4

If you have time, do allow the pork and water chestnuts to mingle with the flavours of the ginger, garlic and soy before cooking. Water chestnuts have a wonderful crunchy texture and although they have little taste of their own they readily absorb the flavours of the marinade.

350 g (12 oz) pork tenderloin
170 g (6 oz) can water chestnuts, drained and sliced
1 clove garlic, crushed
2.5 cm (1 inch) piece fresh root ginger, grated
2 tablespoons Worcestershire sauce
2 tablespoons soy sauce
½ head Chinese leaf, shredded
1 tablespoon chopped coriander leaves
2 teaspoons snipped chives
5 tablespoons light olive oil
1 red pepper, cored, seeded and cut into strips
2 tablespoons sherry or wine vinegar
½ teaspoon dark soft brown sugar
salt and pepper to taste

1 Slice the pork thinly and place in a bowl with the water chestnuts. Add the garlic, ginger, Worcestershire and soy sauces and stir well to coat. Leave to marinate for 20 minutes, or longer.

2 In another bowl toss the Chinese leaf with the chopped coriander leaves and the chives. Arrange on individual plates.

3 Heat 3 tablespoons oil in a wok. Add the pork mixture and stir fry over a high heat to seal. Add the red pepper and continue cooking for a further 2 minutes, until the pork is cooked through. Stir in the remaining oil, vinegar, sugar and seasoning. Spoon over the Chinese leaf and serve.

ABOVE: PORK WITH WATER CHESTNUTS *BELOW:* PORK FILLET WITH BABY CORN

PORK WITH PEANUT SAUCE

SERVES 4

Strips of pork and red pepper in a rich peanut sauce. Serve with rice or orso – tiny rice-shaped pasta – and a simple salad.

3 tablespoons groundnut oil
500 g (1 lb) boneless pork steaks, cut into strips
1 onion, chopped
1 red pepper, cored, seeded and thinly sliced
1 clove garlic, crushed
2.5 cm (1 inch) piece fresh root ginger, grated
2 teaspoons ground coriander
1/2-1 teaspoon ground cumin
2 tablespoons soft dark brown sugar
grated rind and juice of 1 lemon
4 tablespoons crunchy peanut butter
3 tablespoons dark soy sauce
1 tablespoon Worcestershire sauce
salt and pepper to taste

TO GARNISH
chopped parsley or coriander

1 Heat the oil in a wok or sauté pan. Add the pork and stir fry for 1-2 minutes to seal. Add the onion, red pepper, garlic, ginger and spices and cook for a further 3 minutes, stirring constantly.

2 Add the remaining ingredients to the pan and stir well to mix. Lower the heat, cover and simmer for about 20 minutes until the pork is tender.

3 Serve sprinkled with parsley or coriander.

CHILLI PORK

SERVES 4

A South American style dish – best served with rice and a green vegetable. Fried plantain makes a delicious accompaniment.

3 tablespoons groundnut oil
625 g (1 1/4 lb) pork fillet (tenderloin), cubed
1 small onion, chopped
1 clove garlic, crushed
2.5 cm (1 inch) piece fresh root ginger, grated
2 teaspoons mild chilli powder
1/2 teaspoon paprika
2 thyme sprigs
1 tablespoon plain flour
2 tablespoons tomato purée
150 ml (1/4 pint) hot stock
salt and pepper to taste

TO GARNISH
herb sprigs

1 Heat the oil in a wok or sauté pan. Add the pork and stir fry for 1-2 minutes to seal. Add the onion, garlic, ginger, chilli powder, paprika and thyme and continue stir frying for 2 minutes, or until the onion is softened.

2 Add the flour to the pan and cook for 2 minutes, stirring constantly. Stir in the tomato purée and remove from the heat. Gradually stir in the stock. Return to the heat and cook, stirring constantly, until the sauce is smooth and thickened. Cover and cook gently for 15 minutes.

3 Discard the thyme and check the seasoning before serving, garnished with herbs.

PORK WITH NOODLES & MANGETOUT

SERVES 4

Wind-dried Chinese sausages are available from oriental food stores. If you include one in this recipe, use the smaller quantity of pork.

175 g (6 oz) medium egg noodles
2 tablespoons groundnut oil
350-500 g (12 oz-1 lb) pork fillet (tenderloin), thinly sliced
1 clove garlic, crushed
2.5 cm (1 inch) piece fresh root ginger, grated
1 dried Chinese sausage, thinly sliced (optional)
4 spring onions, white part only, chopped
½ red pepper, cored, seeded and cut into diamonds
125 g (4 oz) mangetout
1 teaspoon cornflour
2 tablespoons soy sauce
2 tablespoons sherry
1 tablespoon wine vinegar
salt and pepper to taste

1 Cook the noodles in boiling water according to packet instructions. Drain.

2 Meanwhile, heat the oil in a wok. Add the pork and garlic and stir fry over a high heat for 1 minute to seal.

3 Add the ginger, Chinese sausage if using, spring onions, red pepper and mangetout to the wok and stir fry for 2 minutes.

4 Blend the cornflour with the soy sauce, sherry, vinegar and 2 tablespoons water. Add to the wok and stir until thickened. Cook for 2 minutes. Add the noodles and toss well. Season and serve at once.

ITALIAN SAUSAGE WITH GREEN LENTILS

SERVES 4

Buy fresh Italian sausages such as salamelle, salsicce and cotechino from Italian delicatessens and large supermakets. Be sure to use green or continental lentils as they can be cooked without soaking and retain their texture during cooking.

350 g (12 oz) fresh Italian-style spicy sausages
2 tablespoons virgin olive oil
1 large onion, chopped
1 stick celery, chopped
1 clove garlic, chopped
300 g (10 oz) green lentils
350 g (12 oz) tomatoes, skinned and chopped
3 oregano sprigs
150 ml (¼ pint) dry white wine
salt and pepper to taste
1 tablespoon chopped parsley

1 Prick the sausages all over with a fork and cook uncovered in a large sauté pan with a lid or wo for 3-5 minutes until lightly browned. Transfer to a plate using a slotted spoon and set aside.

2 Add the oil to the pan, then add the onion, celery and garlic and stir fry for 3 minutes until softened. Stir in the lentils, tomatoes, oregano, white wine and seasoning. Cover and cook gently for 15 minutes, stirring twice.

3 Cut the sausages diagonally into thick slices. Stir the parsley into the lentil mixture and scatter th sausages over the top. Cover and cook for 10 minute or until the lentils are just tender and the sausages are hot and cooked through. Serve with crusty breac

CALVES LIVER WITH MUSTARD SEEDS & ROSEMARY

SERVES 4

A simple dish of calves liver and onion flavoured with mustard and rosemary. Take care to avoid overcooking the liver or its creamy texture will be lost – it should be just pink on the inside. Serve with new potatoes and french beans, or pasta and a crisp green salad.

500 g (1 lb) calves liver, thinly sliced
salt and pepper to taste
2 tablespoons olive oil
25 g (1 oz) butter
1 shallot, chopped
1 small onion, sliced
4-5 teaspoons mustard seeds
2 tablespoons finely chopped rosemary

TO GARNISH
rosemary sprigs

1 Season the liver with salt and pepper. Heat the oil and half of the butter in a large frying pan. Add the liver slices and cook for 2-3 minutes each side. Transfer to a serving dish using a slotted spoon and keep warm.

2 Add the shallot and onion to the pan juices and cook for 3 minutes to soften. Add the remaining butter, mustard seeds and chopped rosemary and heat until sizzling. Spoon over the liver and serve at once, garnished with rosemary sprigs.

MEATBALLS IN CREAM & HERB SAUCE

SERVES 4

MEATBALLS
350 g (12 oz) lean minced beef, or veal
125 g (4 oz) back bacon, derinded and chopped
1 small onion, very finely chopped
2 cloves garlic, crushed
125 g (4 oz) pitted black olives
1 tablespoon chopped parsley
1 tablespoon Worcestershire sauce
1 egg yolk
salt and pepper to taste

TO FINISH
1½ tablespoons olive oil
25 g (1 oz) butter
5 tablespoons light stock
3 tablespoons chopped mixed herbs, e.g. parsley and fennel
5 tablespoons double cream

TO GARNISH
fennel or parsley sprigs

1 In a large bowl, mix together all the ingredients for the meatballs. Shape into small balls.

2 Heat the oil and butter in a large frying pan and fry the meatballs, turning constantly, for about 5 minutes until evenly browned. Remove from pan.

3 Add the stock and herbs to the pan, stirring to scrape up any sediment. Cook over a high heat until reduced to about 3 tablespoons. Stir in the cream and seasoning.

4 Return the meatballs to the pan and cook gently for 3-5 minutes. Serve garnished with fennel and accompanied by noodles.

BEEF WITH MINT & CASHEWS

SERVES 4

The coolness of the mint counteracts the fire of the chilli in this stir fry of rump steak and cashew nuts.

2 tablespoons groundnut oil
1 clove garlic, crushed
500 g (1 lb) rump steak, cut into thin strips
1-2 red chillis, seeded and sliced
4 spring onions, sliced
2.5 cm (1 inch) piece fresh root ginger, grated
3 tablespoons dark soy sauce
2 tablespoons sherry
2 tablespoons chopped mint
50 g (2 oz) salted cashew nuts
pepper to taste

TO GARNISH
mint sprigs

1. Heat the oil in a wok. Add the garlic and steak strips and stir fry over a high heat for 1-2 minutes to seal.

2. Add the chillis, spring onions and ginger and stir fry for 1 minute.

3. Add the remaining ingredients and continue stir frying for 1 minute. Season with pepper and serve at once, garnished with mint.

BEEF WITH PEPPERS & NOODLES

SERVES 4

A delicious dish with a Thai influence. If time, pop the beef in the freezer for 30 minutes before cutting; you will find it easier to slice into wafer-thin strips.

250 g (8 oz) egg noodles
2 tablespoons groundnut oil
350 g (12 oz) fillet steak, cut into thin strips
1 small red pepper, cored, seeded and cut into julienne strips
1 small yellow pepper, cored, seeded and cut into julienne strips
salt and pepper to taste

HOT PASTE
2 garlic cloves, chopped
5 cm (2 inch) piece fresh root ginger, chopped
3 stalks lemon grass, bulb end only, chopped (optional)
2 tablespoons groundnut oil
1 teaspoon sesame oil
2 tablespoons soy sauce
3 tablespoons sweet chilli sauce

1. Put all the ingredients for the hot paste in a blender or food processor and process until fairly smooth; or use a pestle and mortar. Set aside.

2. Cook the noodles in boiling water according to packet instructions and drain well.

3. Meanwhile heat the oil in a wok. Add the beef and peppers and stir fry for 3 minutes. Remove from the wok and set aside.

4. Add the hot paste to the wok and cook for 1-2 minutes. Add the noodles, with the beef and pepper mixture, and seasoning. Toss well and heat through. Serve at once.

ABOVE: BEEF WITH PEPPERS & NOODLES *BELOW*: BEEF WITH MINT & CASHEWS

LAMB WITH CORIANDER & LIME

SERVES 4

You can make this very simple stir fry either with loin or neck lamb fillet. Neck fillet is less expensive and readily available, but not as lean and tender as loin. Serve with rice.

3 tablespoons virgin olive oil
350 g (12 oz) fillet of lamb, sliced
1-2 cloves garlic, crushed
¼ teaspoon ground cumin
1 onion, cut into wedges
juice of 2 limes
150 g (5 oz) natural yogurt
3 tablespoons chopped coriander leaves
½ teaspoon sugar
salt and pepper to taste

TO GARNISH
lime slices and coriander leaves

1 Heat the oil in a wok or large frying pan. Add the lamb and garlic and stir fry for 1 minute to seal. Add the cumin and onion and stir fry for 2 minutes.

2 Add the remaining ingredients to the pan. Cook, stirring, for 2-3 minutes until the lamb is tender.

3 Season and serve at once, garnished with lime slices and coriander.

LAMB WITH CHICK PEAS & MINT

SERVES 4

To ensure that this dish is richly flavoured and not too liquid, reduce the sauce right down. Serve with rice or naan bread, or both.

3 tablespoons olive oil
500 g (1 lb) lean leg of lamb, diced
2 onions, chopped
2 cloves garlic, crushed
1 green chilli, seeded and chopped
2 teaspoons coriander seeds, lightly crushed
1 teaspoon cumin seeds, lightly crushed
¼ teaspoon ground allspice
½ teaspoon turmeric
300 ml (½ pint) hot lamb stock
400 g (14 oz) can chick peas, drained
2 tomatoes, skinned and quartered
2 tablespoons chopped mint
salt and pepper to taste

TO SERVE
mint sprigs to garnish
thick natural yogurt

1 Heat the oil in a wok or large sauté pan. Add the lamb and stir fry for about 4 minutes until sealed and browned. Add the onions, garlic, chilli and spices and cook, stirring, for 3 minutes.

2 Add the stock and chick peas to the pan and bring to the boil. Lower the heat, cover and simmer for about 20 minutes until the lamb is tender.

3 Remove the lid and continue cooking until most of the liquid is evaporated. Stir in the tomatoes, mint and seasoning. Cook for a further 2 minutes. Serve garnished with mint and accompanied by rice and thick yogurt.

ABOVE: LAMB WITH CHICK PEAS & MINT BELOW: LAMB WITH CORIANDER & LIME

VEGETABLES

Stir frying is a superb way of cooking vegetables. They retain their crispness, colours stay bright and nutrients are not lost in a sea of cooking water. Choose crisp, fresh vegetables for stir fries and cook them as soon as possible after cutting.

The Chinese and Japanese take great care over the preparation of their vegetables – cutting them into intricate shapes. It's well worth considering visual appeal – even for simple stir fries. Aim to achieve an attractive variety of shapes, colours and textures for maximum effect.

CONTENTS

GREEN VEGETABLE STIR FRY

SERVES 4-6

A fresh tasting mixed vegetable stir fry that can accompany any meal. For a pretty effect, remove lengthwise strips of peel from the cucumber with a canelle knife before slicing.

½ cucumber
3 tablespoons groundnut oil
1 teaspoon sesame oil
½ clove garlic, crushed
2.5 cm (1 inch) piece fresh root ginger, grated
1 stalk lemon grass (optional)
250 g (8 oz) broccoli florets, halved
1 courgette, thinly sliced
125 g (4 oz) mangetout
3 spring onions, shredded
salt and pepper to taste

1 Slice the cucumber fairly thinly and set aside.

2 Heat the oils in a wok. Add the garlic and ginger and stir fry for a few seconds. Grate the bulb end only of the lemon grass, if using, and add to the wok with the broccoli, courgette, mangetout and spring onions. Stir fry for 2-3 minutes.

3 Add the cucumber to the wok and stir fry for a few seconds to heat through. Season with salt and pepper and serve at once.

CHILLI CORN COBS WITH TOMATO

SERVES 4

Sweet chilli sauce is available in bottles – like ketchup – from supermarkets and oriental food stores. Turn this recipe into a delicious main course, if you like, by adding either strips of chicken breast or prawns.

2 tablespoons groundnut oil
2 teaspoons sesame oil
1 clove garlic, crushed
2.5 cm (1 inch) piece fresh root ginger, grated
250 g (8 oz) baby corn cobs
2 tablespoons sweet chilli sauce
1 tablespoon light soy sauce
1 tablespoon sherry
1 teaspoon sugar
4 tomatoes, skinned and cut into wedges
4 spring onions, shredded
salt and pepper to taste

1 Heat the oils in a wok. Add the garlic, ginger and corn cobs and stir fry for 3 minutes.

2 Add the remaining ingredients and stir fry for 2-3 minutes, until the corn cobs are tender. Add seasoning and serve immediately.

ABOVE: CHILLI CORN COBS WITH TOMATO *BELOW*: GREEN VEGETABLE STIR FRY

AUBERGINE IN OYSTER SAUCE

SERVES 3-4

If possible, use crushed Szechwan peppercorns to season this delicious dish. They impart a distinctive aromatic flavour.

1 large aubergine
1 red onion
3 tablespoons groundnut oil
2 teaspoons sesame oil
1 clove garlic, crushed
2 spring onions, sliced diagonally
2 tablespoons oyster sauce
150 ml (¼ pint) chicken stock
1 teaspoon cornflour
salt and pepper (preferably Szechwan) to taste

1 Thinly slice the aubergine. Cut the red onion into wedges and separate the layers into petals.

2 Heat the oils in a wok. Add the garlic, spring onions, aubergine and red onion and stir fry for 3 minutes. Add the oyster sauce and stock and cook for 1-2 minutes.

3 Mix the cornflour to a paste with 1 tablespoon cold water, add to the wok and stir until thickened. Cook for 2 minutes or until the aubergine is tender. Season with salt and pepper. Serve at once.

BABY CORN & MUSHROOM STIR FRY

SERVES 4

This fresh lemony stir fry is an ideal accompaniment to seafood and rich meats, such as duck and pork.

1½ teaspoons fennel seeds
250 g (8 oz) baby corn cobs
1 small red onion
350 g (12 oz) mixed mushrooms, e.g. oyster, shiitake, chestnut, small cup or button
½ cucumber
3 tablespoons groundnut oil
½ clove garlic, crushed
215 g (7 oz) can straw mushrooms, drained
½ teaspoon grated lemon rind
juice of ½ lemon
salt and pepper to taste

1 Put the fennel seeds in a wok over moderate heat and stir for 1-2 minutes until they start to pop; remove and set aside.

2 Leave small corn cobs whole; halve larger ones lengthwise. Cut the onion into wedges and separate into petals. Slice any large mushrooms, otherwise leave whole.

3 Using a canelle knife, cut grooves along the cucumber, then slice fairly thinly.

4 Heat the oil in the wok. Add the garlic and corn cobs and stir fry for 2 minutes. Add the fresh mushrooms and continue stir frying for 2-3 minutes.

5 Stir in the straw mushrooms, lemon rind and juice, onion and cucumber. Stir fry for 1 minute until the mushrooms are tender, but the other vegetables are still slightly crisp; do not overcook. Season with salt and pepper and serve at once, sprinkled with the fennel seeds.

ABOVE: BABY CORN & MUSHROOM STIR FRY *BELOW*: AUBERGINE IN OYSTER SAUCE

SPAGHETTI VEGETABLES WITH ALMONDS

SERVES 4

Shoe-string lengths of carrot, parsnip and courgette with a buttery glaze and toasted almond flakes make an elegant, colourful vegetable accompaniment. Sometimes I use a leek in place of one of the vegetables listed below.

3 medium carrots
2 parsnips
2 courgettes
15 g (½ oz) flaked almonds
2 tablespoons olive oil
small knob of butter
½ teaspoon soft light brown sugar
1 tablespoon lemon juice
salt and pepper to taste

1 Slice the vegetables lengthwise, then cut into long thin julienne or 'spaghetti'.

2 Place the almonds in a wok over a moderate heat and stir until evenly browned; remove and set aside.

3 Heat the oil in the wok, add the vegetables and stir fry for 3 minutes until just tender. Add the butter, sugar and lemon juice and cook, stirring, for 1-2 minutes until glazed.

4 Season with salt and pepper and transfer to a warmed serving dish. Sprinkle with the almonds to serve.

PEPPERS & PERNOD

SERVES 4

Multi-coloured peppers, flavoured with aniseed and fresh basil, are excellent with fish and chicken dishes. This dish may also be chilled and served as a salad accompaniment.

1 each red, green and yellow pepper
2 tablespoons virgin olive oil
3 tablespoons chopped basil
4 tablespoons Pernod, Ouzo or other aniseed liqueur
salt and pepper to taste

TO GARNISH
basil leaves

1 Halve, core, seed and thinly slice the peppers.

2 Heat the oil in a wok or large pan. Add the peppers and stir fry for 3 minutes.

3 Add the basil and Pernod, Ouzo or aniseed liqueur. Cover and cook over a medium heat for 3 minutes, stirring once. Season with salt and pepper. Transfer to a warmed serving dish and garnish with basil leaves to serve.

ABOVE: SPAGHETTI VEGETABLES WITH ALMONDS *BELOW*: PEPPERS & PERNOD

STIR FRIED FENNEL, PEPPERS & WALNUTS

SERVES 4

Serve this tasty stir fry with fish and chicken dishes.

3 tablespoons groundnut oil
1 clove garlic, crushed
1 large fennel bulb, thinly sliced
1 red pepper, cored, seeded and cut into strips
1 yellow pepper, cored, seeded and thinly sliced
4 spring onions, diagonally sliced
50 g (2 oz) walnut pieces
salt and pepper to taste

SAUCE
5 tablespoons chicken stock or water
2 tablespoons light soy sauce
1 teaspoon wine vinegar
1 teaspoon cornflour
pinch of five-spice powder

1 Mix together all the sauce ingredients in a bowl to a smooth paste and set aside.

2 Heat the oil in a wok. Add the garlic, fennel and peppers and stir fry for 2 minutes. Add the spring onions and the walnuts and stir fry for a few seconds.

3 Pour in the sauce mixture, stirring until thickened. Cover and cook over a low heat for 2 minutes. Season and serve at once.

RATATOUILLE

SERVES 6-8

Stir frying is an ideal way to cook substantial servings of this traditional French vegetable dish. Serve it hot as an accompaniment, or cold as a starter or side salad.

1 aubergine, sliced
1 teaspoon salt
3 tablespoons virgin olive oil
2 onions, sliced
2 cloves garlic, crushed
1 red pepper, cored, seeded and thinly sliced
1 green pepper, cored, seeded and thinly sliced
250 g (8 oz) courgettes, sliced
350 g (12 oz) tomatoes, skinned and chopped
1 tablespoon chopped parsley
2 teaspoons chopped thyme
salt and pepper to taste

1 Rinse the aubergine and place in a colander. Sprinkle with the salt and leave to stand for 20 minutes to remove the bitter juices. Rinse thoroughly to remove the salt and drain.

2 Heat the oil in a wok or large frying pan. Add the onions and garlic and stir fry over a medium heat for 3-4 minutes.

3 Add all the remaining ingredients and stir fry for 3 minutes, then cover and cook over a low heat for about 12 minutes until the vegetables are tender. Adjust the seasoning.

GINGERED PARSNIP BATONS

SERVES 4

A delicious accompaniment for roast meats, poultry and game; I particularly like to serve it with duck. As a variation, substitute half the quantity of parsnips with batons of carrot.

500 g (1 lb) parsnips
2 tablespoons olive oil
15 g (½ oz) butter
5 cm (2 inch) piece fresh root ginger, finely
  shredded
1 tablespoon lemon juice
½ teaspoon soft light brown sugar
salt and pepper to taste

TO GARNISH
snipped chives

1 Cut the parsnips in half across the middle, then cut each piece lengthwise into four or six pieces to give batons of approximately equal size.

2 Heat the oil and butter in a wok or large frying pan. Add the ginger and parsnips and stir fry for about 5 minutes, until the parsnips are tender.

3 Add the lemon juice and sugar to the pan and cook for about 1 minute until the parsnips are lightly glazed. Season with salt and pepper.

4 Transfer to a warmed serving dish and sprinkle with snipped chives to serve.

MUSHROOMS WITH MADEIRA & GARLIC

SERVES 4

While developing recipes for a mushroom cookbook, I became addicted to the flavour combination of mushrooms with Madeira wine. This simple vegetable accompaniment is best made using wild field mushrooms, but the large cultivated flat mushrooms available from supermarkets and greengrocers work well too.

50 g (2 oz) butter
1 tablespoon olive oil
2 cloves garlic, thinly sliced
1 shallot, finely chopped
500 g (1 lb) large field mushrooms, thickly sliced
125 ml (4 fl oz) Madeira
1 teaspoon cornflour
salt and pepper to taste

TO GARNISH
parsley sprigs

1 Heat the butter and oil in a wok or large frying pan. Add the garlic and shallot and stir fry for 1 minute. Add the mushrooms and stir fry for a further 2 minutes.

2 Pour in the Madeira, cover and cook over a medium heat for 5 minutes until the mushrooms are tender.

3 Mix the cornflour to a paste with a little cold water, then add to the pan. Stir until thickened. Season with salt and pepper.

4 Transfer to a warmed serving dish and serve at once garnished with parsley.

ABOVE: GINGERED PARSNIP BATONS *BELOW:* MUSHROOMS WITH MADEIRA & GARLIC

ONIONS IN HORSERADISH CREAM

SERVES 4-6

This original stir fry of pearl, red and spring onions with horseradish and a touch of cream is delicious served with seafood and smoked fish, sausages, red meat and chicken. If pearl onions with their characteristic pink-tinged skins are not available, use tiny button onions instead.

250 g (8 oz) pearl onions
1 red onion
6 spring onions
3 tablespoons groundnut oil
2 tablespoons lemon juice
2 tablespoons creamed horseradish
3 tablespoons single cream
salt and pepper to taste

1 Top and tail the pearl onions. Cut the red onion into wedges and separate layers into petals. Cut spring onions diagonally into 5 cm (2 inch) lengths.

2 Heat the oil in a wok or large frying pan. Add the pearl onions and stir fry for 2 minutes. Add the red onion and spring onions and stir fry for a further 2 minutes.

3 Add the lemon juice and creamed horseradish to the wok with 2-3 tablespoons water. Cover and cook for 2 minutes. Stir in the cream and salt and pepper. Serve at once.

BABY ONIONS WITH BACON

SERVES 4-6

A delicious accompaniment for grilled and roast meats. For a richer version, substitute some of the stock with white wine or dry vermouth.

125 g (4 oz) back bacon rashers, derinded and diced
15 g (½ oz) butter
24 small button onions (approximately)
150 ml (¼ pint) light stock or water
4 tablespoons double cream
1 teaspoon chopped thyme
1 teaspoon cornflour
salt and pepper to taste

TO GARNISH
thyme sprigs

1 Cook the bacon in a wok or large frying pan, without additional fat, for 1-2 minutes, until just crisp. Remove with a slotted spoon and set aside.

2 Add the butter to the pan with the onions. Stir fry for 2 minutes, then add the stock or water and return the bacon to the pan. Cover and cook over a medium heat for 5-7 minutes, until the onions are tender. Stir in the cream and thyme.

3 Mix the cornflour to a paste with a little cold water, then add to the pan and stir until thickened. Season with salt and pepper and serve at once, garnished with thyme.

ABOVE: ONIONS IN HORSERADISH CREAM *BELOW*: BABY ONIONS WITH BACON

FRENCH BEAN & MUSHROOM STIR FRY

SERVES 4

Cloud ear mushrooms are not essential to this stir fry, but they add texture. You can buy them dried from Chinese supermarkets, but use sparingly as they grow to huge proportions when soaked!

3 dried cloud ear mushrooms (optional)
3 tablespoons groundnut oil
½ clove garlic, crushed
2.5 cm (1 inch) piece fresh root ginger, grated
1 small leek, thinly sliced
250 g (8 oz) French beans
175 g (6 oz) small open cup mushrooms
2 tablespoons yellow bean sauce or paste
1 tablespoon light soy sauce
pepper to taste

1 If using cloud ear mushrooms, place in a small bowl, cover with boiling water and leave to soak for 20 minutes. Drain, reserving 5 tablespoons liquid. Cut the mushrooms into bite-sized pieces.

2 Heat the oil in a wok. Add the garlic, ginger, leek and French beans, and stir fry for 2 minutes. Add all the mushrooms and stir fry for 1-2 minutes more.

3 Add the yellow bean paste and soy sauce, together with the reserved mushrooms liquid or 5 tablespoons water. Cover and simmer for 2-3 minutes. Season with pepper and serve immediately.

SWEET & SOUR BEANS

SERVES 4

A delicious combination of mixed beans and tomatoes in a light sweet and sour sauce. If short-sprouted beans are not available, use bean sprouts instead.

3 tablespoons groundnut oil
½ clove garlic, crushed
250 g (8 oz) green beans, halved
215 g (7 oz) can red kidney beans, drained
4 tomatoes, skinned and quartered
3 spring onions, shredded
75 g (3 oz) short-sprouted beans
salt and pepper to taste

SAUCE
3 tablespoons light soy sauce
3 tablespoons wine vinegar
3 tablespoons sherry
1 tablespoon clear honey
2 tablespoons soft light brown sugar
6 tablespoons water
1 teaspoon cornflour

1 Mix together all the sauce ingredients in a bowl to a smooth paste and set aside.

2 Heat the oil in a wok. Add the garlic and green beans and stir fry for 1 minute. Add the remaining ingredients and stir fry for 2 minutes.

3 Pour in the sauce mixture, stirring until thickened. Cover and cook gently for 2 minutes. Season with salt and pepper and serve at once.

SPICED CAULIFLOWER, SPINACH & POTATO

SERVES 4-6

Serve with simply grilled chicken or meat, or as part of an Indian meal.

500 g (1 lb) small new potatoes, halved
½ cauliflower, divided into florets
3 tablespoons olive oil
25 g (1 oz) butter
1 clove garlic, crushed
1 large red chilli, sliced and seeded
1 teaspoon cumin seeds, lightly crushed
1 teaspoon coriander seeds, lightly crushed
1 teaspoon mustard seeds, lightly crushed
1 teaspoon garam masala
pinch of turmeric
125 g (4 oz) spinach, finely shredded
salt and pepper to taste

1. Parboil the new potatoes in boiling salted water for 5-6 minutes, then drain.

2. Meanwhile, in a separate pan parboil the cauliflower for 3-4 minutes. Drain thoroughly.

3. Heat the oil and butter in a wok or large frying pan. Add the garlic, chilli and spices and stir fry for a few seconds. Add the potatoes and cauliflower and stir fry for about 4 minutes, until the vegetables are just tender.

4. Add the spinach to the wok and toss lightly to mix. Leave on the heat just long enough for the spinach to wilt. Season and serve immediately.

FIVE SPICED CHINESE LEAF

SERVES 4-6

This tasty stir fry featuring light Chinese leaf and crisp water chestnuts makes a good accompaniment. You can use pak choi or Chinese cabbage instead of the more lettuce-like Chinese leaf.

2 tablespoons groundnut oil
1 teaspoon sesame oil
2.5 cm (1 inch) piece fresh root ginger, grated
large pinch of five-spice powder
215 g (7 oz) can water chestnuts, drained and sliced
2 tablespoons sherry or sake (rice wine)
1 tablespoon soy sauce
½ teaspoon soft light brown sugar
1 head Chinese leaf, roughly torn
salt and pepper to taste

TO GARNISH
coriander leaves

1. Heat the oils in a wok. Add the ginger, five-spice powder and water chestnuts and stir fry for 2 minutes. Stir in the sherry or sake, soy sauce and sugar.

2. Add the Chinese leaf to the wok and stir fry for about 2 minutes, until the leaves are slightly wilted but the white stalks are still crisp. Season with salt and pepper and serve at once, garnished with coriander leaves.

OKRA WITH MUSTARD

SERVES 4-6

Okra features mainly in African, Indian, South American and West Indian cooking. Serve this dish as an accompaniment to poultry and meat dishes, especially lamb.

500 g (1 lb) okra
juice of 1 lemon
3 teaspoons mustard seeds
3 tablespoons olive oil
½ onion, chopped
2 tablespoons mild mustard
3 tablespoons single cream
salt and pepper to taste

TO GARNISH
mint sprigs

1 Top and tail the okra and place in a bowl. Add cold water to cover and half the lemon juice. Leave to stand for about 20 minutes to remove some of the sticky gum. Rinse thoroughly and pat dry.

2 Place the mustard seeds in a wok or large frying pan over moderate heat and stir for about 1 minute to release the flavour. Remove and set aside.

3 Heat the oil in the wok or pan, add the okra and onion and stir fry for 3-4 minutes until tender.

4 Add the mustard and remaining lemon juice to the pan and continue cooking for 1-2 minutes. Stir in the cream, heat gently and season.

5 Transfer to a warmed serving dish and sprinkle with the mustard seeds. Garnish with mint sprigs to serve.

SPICED PLANTAIN

SERVES 4-6

Buy your plantains from large supermarkets or Asian or West Indian stores. Select those which are well speckled with black to ensure they are ripe enough for this recipe. Serve with grilled or barbecued foods for a taste of the Caribbean!

500-625 g (1-1¼ lb) plantains
25 g (1 oz) butter
1 tablespoon olive oil
2.5 cm (1 inch) piece fresh root ginger, shredded
1 tablespoon lemon or lime juice
½-1 teaspoon mild chilli powder
salt to taste

TO GARNISH
lemon slices and thyme sprigs

1 Cut the plantains into wedges or chips approximately 5 cm (2 inches) long.

2 Heat the butter and oil in a wok or large frying pan. Add the plantains and ginger and stir fry for 4-5 minutes, until the plantains are crisp and golden on the outside and soft within.

3 Add the lemon or lime juice and chilli powder to taste and cook for 1 minute. Season with salt and serve hot, garnished with lemon slices and thyme sprigs.

RICE & NOODLES

Rice and noodles are simply delicious stir
fried with a well flavoured oil and a
handful of freshly chopped herbs or toasted
nuts. Include meat, fish, eggs or vegetables
and you can turn exciting accompaniments
into substantial main courses.

Although I've specified which type of rice
or noodles to use in each of these recipes,
you can interchange them as you wish, to suit
your preference. For best results make sure
that cooked rice and noodles are thoroughly
drained before adding to the stir fry.

CONTENTS

FRIED RICE WITH SMOKED HAM & LETTUCE

SERVES 4

This easy rice dish goes particularly well with chicken dishes. You can, of course, use plain roast ham instead of smoked but the flavour will not be quite as good.

25 g (1 oz) butter
2 eggs, beaten
2 tablespoons groundnut oil
4 spring onions, sliced
125 g (4 oz) smoked ham, cut into strips
½ cos lettuce, shredded
2 tablespoons light soy sauce
250 g (8 oz) white rice, cooked
salt and pepper to taste

1 Melt half of the butter in a small saucepan. Add the eggs and scramble lightly until soft and creamy. Set aside.

2 Heat the remaining butter and the oil in a wok. Add the spring onions and ham and stir fry for 1 minute. Stir in the lettuce and soy sauce.

3 Add the rice to the wok together with the scrambled egg and heat through, stirring to prevent sticking. Season with salt and pepper and serve at once.

MUSHROOM & NUT FRIED RICE

SERVES 4-6

Serve as an accompaniment to Chinese dishes, or as a vegetarian lunch with a salad.

5 dried Chinese mushrooms (optional)
3 tablespoons groundnut or olive oil
1 small onion, chopped
175 g (6 oz) button mushrooms, halved
1 clove garlic, crushed
2.5 cm (1 inch) piece fresh root ginger, grated
50 g (2 oz) mangetout
½ red pepper, cored, seeded and cut into thin
    strips
250 g (8 oz) brown rice, cooked
40 g (1½ oz) brazil nuts, sliced
50 g (2 oz) salted cashews
3 tablespoons light soy sauce
salt and pepper to taste

TO GARNISH
coriander sprigs

1 If using the dried mushrooms, soak in boiling water to cover for 20 minutes. Drain, reserving 5 tablespoons water. Discard the stalks and slice the mushroom caps.

2 Heat the oil in a wok. Add the onion, button mushrooms, garlic and ginger and stir fry for 2 minutes. Add the mangetout, red pepper and Chinese mushrooms, if using, and stir fry for 1 minute.

3 Add the rice and nuts to the wok, together with the soy sauce, enough of the reserved mushroom liquid (or water) to moisten, and seasoning. Heat through, stirring to prevent sticking, and serve garnished with coriander.

ABOVE: FRIED RICE WITH SMOKED HAM & LETTUCE   *BELOW*: MUSHROOM & NUT FRIED RICE

ASPARAGUS & EGG RICE

SERVES 4

If fine asparagus is not available use the larger variety, peeling the stalks and slicing them lengthwise but leaving the tips intact. Serve as an accompaniment to fish, seafood and chicken dishes.

15 g (½ oz) butter
2 eggs, beaten
250 g (8 oz) fine asparagus
2 tablespoons olive oil
50 g (2 oz) frozen petits pois, thawed
250 g (8 oz) white rice, cooked
2 tablespoons chopped parsley or chives
salt and pepper to taste

TO GARNISH
chives

1 Heat the butter in a small saucepan. Add the eggs and scramble lightly until soft and creamy. Set aside.

2 Snap off and discard the woody ends of the asparagus. Cut into 5 cm (2 inch) lengths.

3 Heat the oil in a wok. Add the asparagus and stir fry for 2 minutes. Add the peas and stir fry for a further 1 minute.

4 Add the rice and parsley or chives, together with the scrambled egg. Heat through, stirring to prevent sticking. Add seasoning and serve garnished with chives.

EGG FRIED RICE WITH GLAZED VEGETABLES

SERVES 4-6

Glazed vegetable sticks give this simple egg fried rice a delicious sweet flavour. I like to serve it with beef recipes and hot and sour dishes.

1 large carrot
1 parsnip
2 celery sticks
40 g (1½ oz) butter
2 eggs, beaten
2 tablespoons oil
½ teaspoon soft light brown sugar
250 g (8 oz) white or brown rice, cooked
1 tablespoon chopped parsley
salt and pepper to taste

TO GARNISH
chervil or parsley sprigs

1 Cut the carrot, parsnip and celery sticks into julienne (matchstick) strips.

2 Melt 15 g (½ oz) of the butter in a small pan. Add the eggs and scramble lightly until they are soft and creamy. Set aside.

3 Heat the remaining butter and 1 tablespoon oil in a wok. Add the vegetables and stir fry for 2 minutes. Stir in the sugar and cook over a high heat for 1-2 minutes until the vegetables are tender, glazed and just beginning to brown. Transfer to a bowl and keep warm.

4 Heat the remaining 1 tablespoon oil in the wok. Add the rice and heat through, stirring to prevent sticking. Fold in the scrambled egg, parsley and glazed vegetables. Season and serve at once, garnished with chervil or parsley.

SPICED RICE WITH OKRA & CHICKEN

SERVES 4

When buying okra choose small bright green pods, about 7.5-10 cm (3-4 inches) long. Salting and draining removes their sticky gum.

175 g (6 oz) okra
2 teaspoons salt
1 boneless chicken breast, skinned and diced
1 tablespoon Worcestershire sauce
few drops of Tabasco sauce
1 clove garlic, crushed
1/4 teaspoon celery seed
4 tablespoons olive oil
75 g (3 oz) frozen sweetcorn kernels, thawed
250 g (8 oz) white rice, cooked
salt and pepper to taste

1 Top and tail the okra, slice into rings and place in a colander or sieve. Rinse well and sprinkle with the salt. Leave to drain for 15 minutes, then rinse thoroughly to remove the salt. Dry on kitchen paper.

2 Meanwhile, mix together the chicken, Worcestershire sauce, Tabasco, garlic and celery seed.

3 Heat the oil in a wok. Add the chicken mixture and stir fry for 1 minute. Add the okra and continue stir frying for 1 minute, then add the sweetcorn and cook for a further 1 minute.

4 Fold in the rice and heat through, stirring to prevent sticking. Season and serve immediately.

SWEET & SOUR NOODLES

SERVES 4

250 g (8 oz) thread egg noodles
3 tablespoons groundnut oil
1 clove garlic, crushed
2.5 cm (1 inch) piece fresh root ginger, grated
1 small leek, sliced
1 carrot, cut into strips
125 g (4 oz) baby corn cobs, halved
1/2 red pepper, cut into diamonds
2 tomatoes, cut into wedges
1 tablespoon chopped coriander leaves
salt and pepper to taste

SAUCE
3 tablespoons soy sauce
3 tablespoons wine vinegar
3 tablespoons sherry
3 tablespoons soft light brown sugar
6 tablespoons pineapple juice
1 teaspoon cornflour

TO GARNISH
coriander sprigs

1 Mix all the ingredients for the sauce together in a small bowl. Set aside. Cook the noodles according to packet instructions.

2 Heat the oil in a wok. Add the garlic, ginger, leek, carrot, baby corn and red pepper and stir fry over a high heat for 2 minutes.

3 Add the sauce and stir until thickened. Lower the heat and simmer for 2 minutes.

4 Drain the noodles and add to the wok with the tomato wedges and coriander. Toss gently and season. Serve immediately, garnished with coriander.

SINGAPORE NOODLES

SERVES 4-6

Serve as a light meal or tasty accompaniment to oriental dishes. To make the carrot slices an attractive shape, cut lengthwise grooves along the carrot at regular intervals before slicing.

250 g (8 oz) medium egg noodles
3 tablespoons groundnut oil
1 teaspoon sesame oil
1 clove garlic, crushed
1 carrot, thinly sliced
50 g (2 oz) cooked ham, cut into strips
75 g (3 oz) peeled prawns
75 g (3 oz) frozen petits pois, thawed
6 peeled water chestnuts, sliced
3 spring onions, sliced
50 g (2 oz) bean sprouts
125 ml (4 fl oz) chicken stock
2 tablespoons soy sauce
2 teaspoons cornflour
salt and pepper to taste

1 Cook the egg noodles according to the packet instructions.

2 Meanwhile, heat the oils in a wok. Add the garlic and carrot and stir fry for 2 minutes. Add the ham, prawns, peas, water chestnuts, spring onions and bean sprouts and stir fry for 1 minute.

3 Stir in the chicken stock and soy sauce and bring to the boil. Blend the cornflour with 2 tablespoons cold water and add to the wok. Cook, stirring, until thickened.

4 Drain the noodles thoroughly and add to the wok. Heat through, tossing well. Season and serve at once.

HERB & SESAME NOODLES

SERVES 3-4

This fragrant dish of noodles dressed with sesame and herbs is a wonderfully simple accompaniment. Vary the herbs to suit your taste and menu.

175 g (6 oz) instant egg noodles
2 tablespoons sesame oil
2 tablespoons sesame seeds
1/2 clove garlic, crushed
2 tablespoons chopped coriander, basil or mint (or a mixture)
salt and pepper to taste

TO GARNISH
coriander or parsley leaves

1 Cook the egg noodles according to the packet instructions.

2 Meanwhile, heat the oil in a wok, add the sesame seeds and fry for about 30 seconds. Stir in the garlic and herbs.

3 Drain the noodles thoroughly and add to the wok. Heat through tossing well together. Season with salt and pepper and serve at once, garnished with coriander or parsley.

ABOVE: HERB & SESAME NOODLES *BELOW*: SINGAPORE NOODLES

NOODLES WITH AUBERGINE

SERVES 4-6

Serve as an accompaniment to chicken, beef, duck or lamb. Yellow bean sauce or paste and Szechwan peppercorns are available from large supermarkets and oriental food stores.

250 g (8 oz) aubergine
1½ teaspoons salt
250 g (8 oz) thread egg noodles
3-4 tablespoons groundnut oil
1 clove garlic, crushed
½ red pepper, seeded and cut into strips
227 g (8 oz) can bamboo shoots, drained
3 tablespoons yellow bean sauce
¼-½ teaspoon Szechwan peppercorns, crushed
1-2 teaspoons sesame oil

1 Cut the aubergine into strips and place in a colander or sieve. Rinse with cold water, then sprinkle with the salt. Leave to stand for 20 minutes to degorge, then rinse thoroughly and drain well.

2 Cook the egg noodles according to the packet instructions.

3 Meanwhile, heat the groundnut oil in a wok. Add the aubergine, garlic, red pepper and bamboo shoots and stir fry for 2-3 minutes until the aubergine is soft. Add the yellow bean sauce and heat through. Season with Szechwan pepper to taste.

4 Drain the noodles and toss in the sesame oil. Transfer to a warmed serving dish and top with the aubergine mixture to serve.

SCENTED LEMON NOODLES

SERVES 4

Fiery noodles with the Thai flavours of ginger, garlic, chilli and lemon grass – especially good as an accompaniment to fish and chicken dishes.

250 g (8 oz) rice noodles
3 tablespoons olive or groundnut oil
½ clove garlic, crushed
2.5 cm (1 inch) piece fresh root ginger, grated
1 large red or green chilli, seeded and thinly sliced
2 stalks lemon grass (see note)
3 spring onions, sliced
50 g (2 oz) salted peanuts, roughly chopped
salt and pepper to taste

1 Cook the rice noodles according to the packet instructions.

2 Meanwhile, heat the oil in a wok. Add the garlic, ginger and chilli and stir fry for 1 minute.

3 Grate the bulb end of the lemon grass. Add to the wok with the spring onions and peanuts. Continue stir frying for about 30 seconds.

4 Drain the cooked noodles and add to the wok. Heat through, tossing well together. Add seasoning. Serve immediately.

Note If lemon grass is not obtainable, substitute the grated rind and juice of ½ lemon and ½ teaspooon brown sugar.

ABOVE: NOODLES WITH AUBERGINE BELOW: SCENTED LEMON NOODLES

DESSERTS

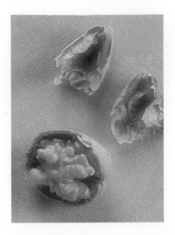

You may be surprised to discover a dessert
chapter in a book on stir frying but, as
vegetables cook so well by this method, I see
no reason why the same technique should not
be used with fresh fruits to create fast, simple
desserts.

Glazing and caramelizing fruit is easy in a
large frying pan or wok, and delicious sauces
can be made in an instant using appropriate
liqueurs and spirits and fresh fruit juices.

CONTENTS

EXOTIC FRUIT STIR FRY

SERVES 4

Exotic fruits such as star fruit, kumquats and pineapple stir fry rather well, staying intact as long as you are fairly gentle. Serve this dessert hot or cold with cream, fromage frais or yogurt, or with melt-in-the-mouth meringues.

40 g (1½ oz) butter
175 g (6 oz) kumquats, halved
2 star fruit, sliced
1 mango, peeled, stoned and sliced
½ small pineapple, peeled, cored and cubed
25-50 g (1-2 oz) soft light brown sugar
juice of 1 lemon
finely grated rind and juice of 1 lime
½ teaspoon cornflour
4 tablespoons Marsala or other sweet wine
edible flowers to decorate (optional)

1 Melt the butter in a wok. Add the fruits and stir fry for 3 minutes. Add the sugar, lemon juice, lime rind and juice, and cook for 2 minutes until the sugar is dissolved.

2 Mix the cornflour to a paste with the Marsala, then add to the wok and cook, stirring gently, until thickened. Serve hot or chilled, sprinkled with edible flowers if available.

CHERRIES IN COINTREAU

SERVES 4

These sweet black cherries in a cointreau-flavoured sauce can be served hot or chilled with ice cream, cream or yogurt and crisp dessert biscuits. I leave the cherries whole so they hold their shape during cooking, but you may prefer to stone them first.

500 g (1 lb) ripe black cherries
25 g (1 oz) caster sugar
1 cinnamon stick
finely grated rind and juice of 1 orange
5 tablespoons cointreau
1 teaspoon cornflour

1 Place the cherries in a wok or large saucepan with the sugar, cinnamon, orange rind and juice and 125 ml (4 fl oz) water. Cook, stirring, over a medium heat for 2-3 minutes until the sugar is dissolved. Lower the heat and simmer for 5 minutes or until the cherries are quite soft but not collapsing; the timing will depend upon the ripeness of the cherries.

2 Stir in the cointreau and heat through. Remove the cherries, using a slotted spoon, and place in a warmed serving dish.

3 Mix the cornflour to a paste with 1 tablespoon cold water. Add to the pan and cook, stirring, until thickened. Pour over the hot cherries. Serve immediately or allow to cool and chill before serving

BANANAS WITH RUM

For an indulgent dessert, serve these delicious bananas with whipped cream or ice cream and brandy snaps. Less sinful people may prefer them with Greek-style yogurt or smetana!

4 large bananas
juice of 1 lemon
40 g (1½ oz) butter
4 tablespoons soft light brown sugar
½ teaspoon ground mixed spice
5 tablespoons dark rum
½ teaspoon cornflour
finely pared and shredded rind and juice of 1
  orange
orange slices to decorate

1 Cut the bananas diagonally into 5 cm (2 inch) lengths. Toss them in the lemon juice to prevent discoloration, then drain well.

2 Heat the butter in a wok or large frying pan. Add the bananas, sugar and spice and stir fry gently for about 2 minutes until beginning to soften. Stir in the rum and cook for a further 1 minute until the bananas are hot and tender.

3 Carefully transfer the bananas to a warmed serving plate using a slotted spoon, leaving the juices in the pan.

4 Mix the cornflour to a paste with the orange juice. Add to the pan with the shredded orange rind and cook, stirring, for 1 minute until thickened. Pour over the bananas and serve immediately, decorated with orange slices.

CARAMELIZED APPLES & PEARS

SERVES 4

I like to serve this dessert with dollops of cream, crème fraîche or thick yogurt – sprinkled with ground cinnamon.

1 lemon
2 dessert apples
3 firm pears
50 g (2 oz) butter
2-3 tablespoons brandy
2-3 tablespoons demerara sugar

1 Using a zester, finely pare the rind from half of the lemon in strips. Shred finely and set aside. Squeeze the juice from the lemon.

2 Peel, halve and core the apples and pears, then cut each into thick wedges. Toss in the lemon juice to prevent discoloration, then drain well on kitchen paper.

3 Heat the butter in a wok or large frying pan, add the fruit and stir fry over a high heat for 2-3 minutes until the apples and pears are golden brown; take care to avoid burning.

4 Sprinkle with the brandy and sugar. Continue to stir fry for about 3 minutes until the fruit is glazed with caramel. Stir in the lemon zest.

5 Serve hot, with cream, crème fraîche or yogurt.

ABOVE: APRICOTS WITH HONEY & ALMONDS (PAGE 94) *CENTRE*: SPICED BANANAS WITH RUM
BELOW: CARAMELIZED APPLES & PEARS

PEAR & APRICOT COMPOTE

SERVES 4

A delicious compote, subtly flavoured with vanilla and topped with pistachio nuts.

TOPPING
15 g (½ oz) butter
25 g (1 oz) shelled pistachio nuts, chopped
finely grated rind of ½ lemon
1 tablespoon caster sugar

COMPOTE
250 g (8 oz) dried pears
250 g (8 oz) no-soak dried apricots
25 g (1 oz) caster sugar
juice of 1 lemon
1 vanilla pod
150 ml (¼ pint) sweet dessert wine

1 For the topping, melt the butter in a small frying pan, add the nuts and fry gently for 2 minutes or until just beginning to brown. Stir in the lemon rind and sugar. Remove from the heat and set aside.

2 Place all the ingredients for the compote in a pan with 5 tablespoons water. Cook gently, stirring until the sugar is dissolved, then cover and allow to simmer for 20 minutes, until the fruit is tender. Remove the lid and boil briskly until the liquid is reduced to a thin syrup. Discard the vanilla.

3 Serve the compote hot or chilled, sprinkled with the pistachio topping and accompanied by cream or yogurt.

PINEAPPLE WITH COCONUT CREAM

SERVES 4

Stem ginger preserved in syrup is available in jars from most supermarkets. Here it is combined with pina colada flavours – pineapple, coconut and cream.

40 g (1½ oz) butter
1 large pineapple, peeled, cored and sliced
3 pieces preserved stem ginger, thinly sliced
2 tablespoons demerara sugar
pinch of ground cinnamon
¼ teaspoon finely grated lemon rind
2 tablespoons white rum
25 g (1 oz) creamed coconut, in pieces
150 ml (¼ pint) double cream
shredded lemon zest and mint sprigs to decorate

1 Melt the butter in a wok. Add the pineapple and ginger and stir fry for 4 minutes. Add the sugar, cinnamon, lemon rind and rum and cook for 2-3 minutes until the sugar is dissolved and the pineapple is tender. Transfer the pineapple and ginger to a serving plate, using a slotted spoon.

2 Boil the cooking juices in the pan until reduced to about 3 tablespoons. Lower the heat, then add the creamed coconut and cook, stirring, until melted. Remove from the heat and leave until cold. Softly whip the cream and fold in the coconut mixture.

3 Spoon the coconut cream on top of the pineapple and sprinkle with the lemon zest. Decorate with mint sprigs.

ABOVE: SCENTED RHUBARB (PAGE 94) *CENTRE*: PEAR & APRICOT COMPOTE
BELOW: PINEAPPLE WITH COCONUT CREAM

APRICOTS WITH HONEY & ALMONDS

SERVES 4-6

You can serve this dish hot or cold, simply with yogurt or fromage frais. Illustrated on page 91.

40 g (1½ oz) split blanched almonds
25 g (1 oz) butter
500 g (1 lb) apricots, halved and stoned
½ teaspoon ground cinnamon
3 tablespoons brandy
3 tablespoons clear honey
mint sprigs to decorate

1 Stir the almonds in a large frying pan or wok over moderate heat until golden brown. Add the butter, apricots and cinnamon and stir fry for 3 minutes.

2 Stir in the brandy and honey and continue cooking for 2 minutes, or until the apricots are just soft.

3 Serve hot or cold, decorated with mint.

SCENTED RHUBARB

SERVES 4

Cardamom adds a wonderful subtle fragrance to this sharp fruit. Serve well chilled with a dollop of clotted cream, mascarpone cheese or thick cream and crisp dessert biscuits. Illustrated on page 93.

750 g (1½ lb) rhubarb
50 g (2 oz) caster sugar
5 green or white cardamom pods
150 ml (¼ pint) sweet dessert wine
mint sprigs to decorate

1 Cut the rhubarb into 4 cm (1½ inch) lengths and place in a large frying pan or sauté pan with the sugar. Cook, over a medium heat, stirring occasionally, for 4-5 minutes until the sugar is dissolved and the pink juices run from the fruit.

2 Meanwhile, crack open the cardamom pods and take out the seeds; discard the pods. Crush the seeds, using a pestle and mortar or rolling pin.

3 Add the crushed cardamom seeds and dessert wine to the pan and bring to the boil. Lower the heat and simmer for 4-5 minutes until the rhubarb is soft but still holding its shape; do not overcook or the fruit will collapse to a pulp.

4 Allow to cool, then chill before serving. Decorate with mint sprigs.

INDEX

M

Mango, chicken and spinach salad 14

Meatballs in cream and herb sauce 48

Monkfish with okra and tomato 20

Mushroom:

  Baby corn and mushroom stir fry 58

  French bean and mushroom stir fry 68

  Mushroom and nut fried rice 76

  Mushrooms with Madeira and garlic 64

Mussels in black bean sauce 18

N

Noodles:

  Beef with peppers and noodles 50

  Chicken stir fry with noodles 38

  Herb and sesame noodles 82

  Noodles with aubergine 84

  Pork with noodles and mangetout 46

  Singapore noodles 82

  Scented lemon noodles 84

  Sweet and sour noodles 80

O

Okra:

  Monkfish with okra and tomato 20

  Okra with mustard 72

  Spiced rice with okra and chicken 80

Onion:

  Baby onions with bacon 66

  Onions in horseradish cream 66

P

Parsnip:

  Gingered parsnip batons 64

Peanut sauce 12

Pear:

  Caramelized apples and pears 90

  Pear and apricot compote 92

Peppers and Pernod 60

Pineapple with coconut cream 92

Plantain:

  Spiced plantain 72

Pork:

  Chilli pork 44

  Pork fillet with baby corn 42

  Pork with noodles and mangetout 46

  Pork with peanut sauce 44

  Pork with water chestnuts 42

Prawn:

  Bacon-wrapped prawn salad 8

  Prawn korma 20

  Quick fried prawns with ginger 18

  Seafood with fennel and tomatoes 24

R

Ratatouille 62

Rhubarb:

  Scented rhubarb 94

Rice:

  Asparagus and egg rice 78

  Egg fried rice with glazed vegetables 78

  Fried rice with smoked ham and lettuce 76

  Mushroom and nut fried rice 76

  Spiced rice with okra and chicken 80

S

Salads:

  Bacon-wrapped prawn salad 8

  Cheese salad with mixed hot nuts 14

  Chicken livers with salad leaves 8

  Gado-gado 12

  Hot bacon and pecan salad 10

Mango, chicken and spinach salad 14

Salami and omelette salad 10

Salmon:

  Caledonian salmon with gingered vegetables 28

Sausage:

  Italian sausage with green lentils 46

Scallops in saffron cream sauce 26

Scented lemon noodles 84

Scented rhubarb 94

Seafood with fennel and tomatoes 24

Singapore noodles 82

Sizzling trout with garlic and spring onions 32

Smoked haddock with spring vegetables 32

Sole:

  Lemon sole and lettuce 22

Spaghetti vegetables with almonds 60

Spiced bananas with rum 90

Spiced cauliflower, spinach and potato 70

Spiced plantain 72

Spiced rice with okra and chicken 80

Sweet and sour beans 68

Sweet and sour fish balls 30

Sweet and sour noodles 80

T

Trout:

  Sizzling trout with garlic and spring onions 32

W

Water chestnut:

  Pork with water chestnuts 42